Ghazalnāma

Ghazalnāma
Poems from Delhi, Belfast, and Urdu

Maaz Bin Bilal

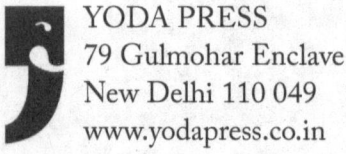
YODA PRESS
79 Gulmohar Enclave
New Delhi 110 049
www.yodapress.co.in

Copyright © Maaz Bin Bilal 2019

The moral rights of the author have been asserted
Database right YODA PRESS (maker)

All rights reserved. Enquiries concerning reproduction outside the scope of the above should be sent to YODA PRESS at the address above.

ISBN 978-93-82579-74-8

Editor in charge: Tanya Singh
Typeset by R. Ajith Kumar
Printed at
Published by Arpita Das for YODA PRESS

To
all my yaars

What is life but the revelation of order among elements?
What is death but a disturbance in the parts?

زندگی کیا ہے عناصر میں ظہور ترتیب
موت کیا ہے ان ہی اجزا کا پریشاں ہونا
—— پنڈت برج نارائن چکبست

—Brij Narāyan Chakbast (1882–1926)

CONTENTS

Preface — xv
The Ghazal in Your Hands

Acknowledgements — xvii

DELHI
1. Ballimaran — 3
2. This Night — 4
3. Restless — 5
4. Knowledge I — 6
5. Scars — 7
6. View from Jama Masjid's Minar — 13
7. Feverish in Delhi in 2010 — 14
8. Knowledge II — 15
9. The L Word — 16
10. If I Could Write this in Fire — 17

BELFAST
11. The Tall and Short of It — 21
12. Biryani in Belfast — 22
13. Belfast/Béal Feirste — 23
14. On Those Nights — 26
15. A Ghazal for Gaza — 27
16. Another Art — 28
17. Two Typos on Facebook — 29
18. The Summit of Cave Hill — 31

URDU

19. Merely a Heart	35
20. Let's Live in that Place	39
21. Thousands of Desires, Such	41
22. Child's Play	45
23. At Every Little Thing	49
24. It Wasn't Our Destiny	53
25. Not a Wish Comes to Fruition	57
26. Being	61
27. To the Rival	63
28. Remembrance	67
29. Holi	69
30. Colour	71
31. The Master of Royals	73
32. The Heart is Asunder	77
33. Somewhat	81
34. Be it Gandhi, Be it Ghalib	85

DELHI AGAIN

35. Air Black	91
36. Muslimah	93
37. To Michelangelo and Aditi Rao	97
38. In His Heart	98
39. Haiku I	100
40. Haiku II	101
41. Stardust	102
42. A Shriek About Kashmir, July 2016	103
43. Let's War, Said He	105
44. The Frogs in her Dreams	107
45. Amaltas–Monsoon	108
46. Agra, 1948	110

47. Lessons in World Geography	112
48. The Law	114
49. Champa	116
50. Night and Day	117
51. Caravans of Love	119
52. Ghazal After Adrienne Rich	121
Endnotes	122
About the Poet	127

Maaz thought he would live happily in Europe,
Did he know he had Delhi's map in his heart?

Ghazalnāma is the verse collection of my experiences in the worlds I have inhabited—cultural and spatial. It is as much a *safarnāma* or travelogue of the mind as it is a collection of ghazals and other poems in translation across different terrains.

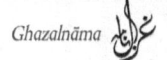

PREFACE

The Ghazal in Your Hands
To Haris Qadeer and Suchismita

> *Two frail arms of your delicate form I pursue,*
> *Inaccessible, vibrant, sublime at the end.*
>   —John Hollander

The ghazal is conversation, mehndi in your hands,
the beauty of a gazelle, coquetry in your hands.

In each couplet, a new thought unravels in paradox,
the heart lies in between the symmetry of your hands.

What more may be said in rhymes and refrains? Entire
cultures—not desolate towns, no folly in your hands.

Many idols are loved and beauty appraised—beloved
boys, girls, and wine. God lives in the paisley in your hands.

Two moments you know: your birth and death; what
weapon better than twin prosody in your hands?

'In chaos, order free verse, not a tight form,' they say,
but you'd capture life here, philosophy in your hands.

Mir and Ghalib gained many a yaar, but it was Faiz
who befriended his raqeeb, the enemy in your hands.

A form thus perfected, will you better Shahid, Maaz?
Let poetry come, become clay, like putty in your hands.

ACKNOWLEDGEMENTS

Ghazalnāma is already dedicated to friends, lovers, and other gods, and many individual poems to friends and writers who directly inspired them. Still, there are others who helped me at various stages of my creative journey and must be acknowledged. The first couplet I remember ever writing and reciting, was in Urdu, at the age of three and under the influence of my father, Bilal Ahmed, who introduced me to poetry, politics, and history. I imagine that he would have appreciated this moment.

Urdu, as a creative language of expression, was left behind, even as it emerges from the subliminal every time in my English verse. I first began writing poetry in English with some degree of serious attention in my BA at Zakir Husain College with the encouragement of my teacher, Dr Sukrita Paul Kumar, and after the scansion class by Ms Rashmi Govind. Working alongside Aruni Kashyap at my craft during MA gave further belief and a sense of what was possible. Dr Ashish Roy showed kind appreciation and awarded me the M. M. Bhalla Poetry Prize at St Stephen's College. Semeen Ali and Nabina Das, fellow poets, were always encouraging, as was Vivek Narayanan in the early days, who would take out time to respond to tentative emails. Ciaran Carson at Queen's University in Belfast minced no words in his critique. My mother often helped with translations, and Prof. Anisur Rehman responded to the early ones with generosity. Uttaran Das Gupta and Suchismita Chattopadhyay were my first readers for many poems here.

Acknowledgements

For *Ghazalnāma*, I cannot thank enough Arpita Das, my publisher, for taking on the project and believing in the work. Gabriel Rosenstock, bilingual poet and translator, who first sought me out with an Irish translation of one of my poems, has been a most large-hearted friend, and very kindly shared his thoughts for this collection. Arundhathi Subramaniam, the forever-young poet I most deeply admire, has overwhelmed me with her kind attentions to my poetry; to her my deepest thanks. Thanks to James Croal Jackson for allowing me to use his photograph, 'Go Your Own Way', and to Adarsh Jogani for the Jama Masjid photograph. Dibyajyoti Sarma suggested a restructuring for the collection that I believe allows for a smoother reading. Tanya Singh at Yoda Press has closely edited the manuscript. R. Ajith Kumar managed to find good control over the bilingual designs. Sarang Sena, childhood friend and photographer extraordinaire, let me reserve the cover photo a couple of years back.

A huge thanks to all editors who first found the poems published here fit for their journals, magazines, and anthologies. But for you, my work may have never seen the light of day. And thanks to all those too who arranged many readings, but for whom the ghazals may not have been heard in the din of the sounds of the Delhi night.

DELHI

دهلی

Ghazalnāma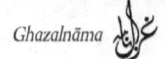

Ballimaran[1]

Said Ghalib,
'twas not his destiny
to be one with his beloved.[2]

My lover too,
lives across his house.
Is it something in the air?

This Night

Many a memory at stake this night.
Do you think of me too, awake, this night?

Shahid stares at me from the book cover,
As I tempt a ghazal to fake this night.

The moon in the sky and I in my bed,
I wish I too could turn a rake this night.

This monsoon, with my tears, the driest ever,
Would your tears for me form a lake this night?

Gave even the echoes of my best poems,
Would I not get one word, to take this night?

One law shouldn't apply to men and lovers,
Will there be born another Blake this night?

Lord made Mi'raj[3] long, so to travel seven skies,
It appears the same God did make this night.

'Ripeness is all' and all time passes.
So too is dawn about to break this night.

Ghalib-o-Faiz couldn't drown grief in ghazals.
Then what Spires, O Maaz, will you Shake this night?

Restless

The promise, forever, there to be, restless.
And nebulous stars' destiny, restless.

Where do I locate her God in this world?
Heisenberg's electrons mutiny, restless.

Shall I fall dead or grieve endlessly?
The wild bees gather their honey, restless.

Metaphors of water, wavy bodies,
Fickle, fluid, flowing in a flurry, restless.

You come not and I keep biding my time.
The peacock's wings are furled, surly, restless.

Together in raging storms, powerless,
Delhi too, romantic, rainy, restless.

What of my love, our passion, your indifference?
The earth, oceans, very heavens break free, restless.

Find meaning in God, her person, in words,
Nestlings call for food, from a tree, restless.

Add on, add on to the surplus worlds,
Who gives a damn, Maaz, that you be restless?

Knowledge I

One day, offended,
I did not speak to you Dad.
I knew it hurt and pained.

But I did not know
that you'd revenge yourself
in absence, never to be spoken to
again.

Scars

I

If only it was
that the sky was not saffron
and the ground not red
and the house, the workshop, the bakery
were not ablaze
in flames that threatened
with more hate than heat,

and had they allowed us
the little green haven,
land,
that we too had nourished,
having wrested it,
from common foes,
with equal gusto.

If only the eye were red
merely of smoke
and my sister dead
of stabs in her back,
just.

Or if, at least,
they had heeded
my folded hands, brown
my head,
bowed in supplication, round,
in entreating
what humanity

a mob may have,
and not chopped it off…
to be soaked
in the fountainhead
of red
that sprung
from my
diminished
corpse,
that did not
immediately fall
as had my head
(not yet knowing
manhood, nor
the sense in it all,
the candles of my
seventh wishes
not yet been thrown away),

then,
when Abbu would come
in three days' time,
we all would welcome him
and
I would run up to him
and jump into his arms
as he'd come,
just as I had asked,
with a plane,
exactly like the one
that made,
on Republic Day,
tricolours
in the sky.

II

This
is what they called
'paradise on earth',
and it was ours
we used to believe,
until,
the day
we first heard
the noise
and went to the square
to behold
that the world
had gone mad,
that it was
black,
and red
made of alien shapes,
and smells.

Smells.
The smells
that smelt
like melting fat
in a pan,
greasy meat frying,
but
if only these too
could be smelt
similarly

with an appetite
that was not to be killed
for ages to come,
smells, that were not
so gross
so revolting
to make us reek of them
bath after
bath, week after
week.

They claimed
Kashmir.
They said it was theirs.
It was
their
right divine.
And so
they were making,
and said,
in future
would make,
more
such noises,
and would create
more
such smells,
everywhere.
Soon it was all over,
over the radio,
the Aakashvani,
and the DD.

Ghazalnāma

Now,

we have live telecasts
of
Kargil and
Kokarnag.
But
that smell has not worn out,
even though today
I live in Delhi.

But so has not,
the one that comes
from the
sandal,
soil,
snow,
saffron, and the
sun that
shines on the
stones of
Shankaracharya Temple, and on
Srinagar and river
Sindhu—
some things that
spell the
summary
of my Kashmir.

Photo Credit: Adarsh Jogani

Ghazalnāma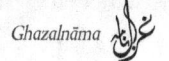

View from Jama Masjid's Minar

Like ants
they seem as I look down from the top,
mostly white, some grey, some black, red even,
creeping from one end to the other
of that large flat courtyard,
itself red,
crawling to their ablutions—their *wuzu*[4]—
and then heading on to the side of the setting sun.

For whom this *sijdah*?
To that hawk-eyed viewer
who sees them
as ants, himself perched
forever at the top?

Feverish in Delhi in 2010

Many reasons to break appointments, feverish,
They rise and fall, the moon's crescents, feverish.

Culture and art galore in our capital,
Delhi dengue from coolers and vents, feverish.

Swank stadia, planters, and sure security,
When on the roads plenty of dents, feverish.

Commonwealth bonhomie, Hiltons and Taj, five-stars,
Hospitals will hold four per berth, feverish.

Youth frenzies for travel, for fun and for outdoors.
Let's go to Triund, spend a night in tents, feverish.

The cosmic is born here in juristic purviews,
New and old legal entities ferment feverish.

Get the energy and desire to challenge verdicts,
Often harmony and peace prevent (the) feverish.

Standards of clothing, set by God, Sangh, and France,
More than costume, the men are rent feverish.

The red man, they say, will be free of all the binds,
Why to that faith, Maaz, not be lent feverish?

Knowledge II

Talab is thirst,
Talib, who seeks,
Taliban are seekers,
traditionally, of knowledge.

These days,
words, as I knew them,
I know, no longer
mean the same.

The L Word

for Ammel

Such epistemic murk around the L word.
Aren't all trying to work around the L word?

No Shireen for me, no Heer, I'm no Qais,
Other desires too lurk around the L word.

Jehangir's City, Shalimar, Anarkali,
Left my heart there to bark around the L word.

Tigresses may take all in Sundarbans,
A male, what use my quirks around the L word?

In Arabic, come seek 'refuge' in Maaz,
What use being a Turk around the L word?

Ghazalnāma

If I Could Write This in Fire[5]

If I could write this in fire
so hot
For it to be etched on the very sinews of your heart
    such that it would be frozen there forever
That it could scorch your eyes
    so no one else, evermore, would you read
    have eyes for no other; the ones that read me last
That it could char your whole skin
        so none would look at you
    and I, only I, remained with your touch
    fragrant with the odour of your sweat
    gleaming in your fiery glow
    rekindling each day in my own sanctuary
    those smouldering coals of lost memories
    reading, re-reading
    such words—
    inflammable

Then, only then, would I say
    Yes, indeed, I can write

BELFAST

بیلفاسٹ

Ghazalnāma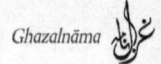

The Tall and Short of It

They grow tall in my country,
The pine and the thorn.

Here, where it is forever
windy and wet,
grass grows, green and short.

Still, dig under the furze,
in both lands, partitioned,
and find you will,
the still-bleeding stigmata, nailed in,
by the Saxon Pilate, the Crown's Nazarene.

Biryani in Belfast

Making biryani in Belfast
is no Trouble.
You get the ready-made Pakistani spice-mix
from the Indian store,
follow the recipe, add some saffron,
and chillies and cardamom,
and wallah, there it is!
The green enmeshed in the orange rice,
even as some grains fail to catch colour,
and remain simply white
—it all smells delicious.
The brown meat is nicely softened,
but also stands out.

Biryani in Belfast

Making biryani in Belfast
is no Trouble.
You get the ready-made Pakistani spice-mix
from the Indian store,
follow the recipe, add some saffron,
and chillies and cardamom,
and wallah, there it is!
The green enmeshed in the orange rice,
even as some grains fail to catch colour,
and remain simply white
—it all smells delicious.
The brown meat is nicely softened,
but also stands out.

Belfast/Béal Feirste

I map anew an old
city. Drafting cartography in verse:
novel speech-acts amidst old nomenclature.
Charting a topical, onomastic flânerie.

For starters,
would you believe, UK's provincial capital
has a Punjab in it?
With its very own ABD:
the Agra, Baroda, and Delhi Streets.
C for Cruelty is now missing.

City-side of the River Lagan, you must cross the deserted
Holylands:
streets monikered Jerusalem, Damascus, Cairo, and Palestine.

Within walking distance lies Empire Street.

It's a side street off Donegall Road.
In Gaelic it's called, 'Dún na nGall'.
'Fort of the foreigners' is what it means.

I am a foreigner here.
My apartment on Sandy Row faces
the Orange Hall. King Billy
was Dutch.

A whole quarter is named after the Queen.
Here I go to school at QUB.
Victoria stands tall,
in front of the City Hall.
But when Lizbeth visits
the hills around still resound,
'Our Queen is Erin.'

Photo Credit: Maaz Bin Bilal

Photo Credit: Maaz Bin Bilal

On those Nights

And I thought we're to agree on those nights.
Find each other, stop being lonely, on those nights.

Smooth-skinned, long-haired, pink thick lips, deep hungry
kisses, was I his fantasy on those nights?

I made love to her in all earnestness,
Seems she wasn't alcohol-free on those nights.

The long walk to Lisburn, a rebuttal,
Go Tesco's, fetch a Christmas tree on those nights.

Cocky, bizarre, unsure and scared, shamming
in theory and psychology, on those nights.

Beauty-beholder, intelligence-perception,
Bingo, handsome-keeper! Shitty on those nights.

Meanings of friendships, philia and eros,
Truth 'conomies in a melee, on those nights.

So will we not talk, see each other, make love?
To her heart was she privy on those nights?

So much delight, 'Here's looking at you, kid,'
Sheer pleasure from you pretty, on those nights.

May you write couplets, do what you may, Maaz,
She's Shiva's triple wife, Shambhavi, on those nights.

A Ghazal for Gaza

for two Mahmouds—Awad and Darwish

*In response to a video of the celebratory chants by some Israelis:
'No Children are left there, Olé, Olé'.*

Four young footballers were playing on the beach,
When men went coursing, preying on the beach.

They built castles high up into the skies,
Those children of Gaza, claying on the beach.

In the grime of their game, in a grain of sand,
All plagues of Egypt, slaying on the beach.

Football cenotaphs in place of their bodies,
Their fathers are now laying on the beach.

Pulped skulls: rubble, debris, spatter, graffiti,
Iron-Dome confetti spraying on the beach.

Sunbathers on that sand? Swimmers in that sea?
Love-making, dilly-dallying, delaying on the beach?

That flotilla of aid, now long-sunk, bled
for stops to bloodlettings, baying on the beach.

We die-in on streets in your New Yorks, your
Londons. Please, no more flaying on the beach.

Poetry's perverse, read Maaz's meagre ghazal,
'No children are left there!' weighing on the beach.

Another Art

for Bishop and Heaney

Loss of originality is a crisis.
In the very use of language that loss
lives. Living is losing, a day, a moment, at a time.
Time, which is not the best or worst,
that is, and produces banal lives.

Aren't old gods lost, whole religions, prophets?
Species, people, science, scripts all die, as shall I.
I lost a father early on, then father-figures, lovers, beloveds,
friends, family, my childhood, my teenage, soon my twenties,
another city,
my job, my hair, my charm, my ambition—losses swell.

A thumb was lost, by my new football friend as a pyrotechnic child,
but he boxes, and blocks goals, like punches, with a squarer fist, as
I hold a pen, tight, in mine, and write to gain loss,
to order chaos, find meaning in the echoes of lines.

Ghazalnāma

Two Typos on Facebook

to Sanjukta and Andrew Eaton

I

The first was a girlfriend's who wrote 'heartarming' to
a post of pictures of brave, path-breaking
women. One lay prostrate on a gargoyle at Empire State,
taking the very first pictures of the new New York.

And women who flew the first planes or fixed railroads when their
men were away at war, or who blew bombs: the first terrorists,
when it was still a good word, and as eighteen-year olds shot
bullets from Barcelona into Franco's fascist heart.

'Heartarming' then, seemed just right,
a fortuitous oversight that armed the heart,
and set it ablaze rather than give a tepid 'warmth'.

II

The second, more recent, a friend who has been
caught, 'waisting time' with an I before the S!
Visions and sights reside in this sleight of fingers
working to redeem themselves on black and white keys.

Imagine taking time to the waist, as his mother,
in a secular Pietà, spanking it as it lies,
etherized, guilty of its vagaries,
of ending species, gods and their mystery.

Or as a lover take time to your waist, make it stand still
in ecstasy, or to the waist, like a friend—the hurtful enemy,
forget its betrayals, crimes, in a mental mime, embrace its apathy.

Photo Credit: James Croal Jackson

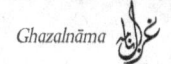

The Summit of Cave Hill

an ekphrastic ghazal after 'Go Your Own Way' by James Croal Jackson
to Ciaran Carson

That picture-perfect mount reminds of the summit of Cave Hill,
Those nostalgic gentle slopes, those binds of the summit of Cave Hill.

In my very first week in Belfast, I climbed up its dirt paths,
Blown away by the views and winds of the summit of Cave Hill.

My historian-guide, with whom I did the hike, spoke highly of
the United Irishmen's keen mind, of the summit of Cave Hill.

A hiker lady found domesticated elephants shady,
Dogs, cats, horses, mules—she did not mind, off the summit of
    Cave Hill.

Short grass on the hill and cirrus clouds in the sky, the Irish sea
isn't in the picture, hidden behind the summit of Cave Hill.

They say the mount's silhouette, inspired Swift to create Gulliver,
Lilliput, Brobdingnag and their kind, off the summit of Cave Hill.

Later, I wrote a poem, 'The Tall and Short of It', compared Ireland
to India, for which I had pined, off the summit of Cave Hill.

I took it to a local poetry group, they dissed its grassy tropes,
To comparative poetics—disinclined, off the summit of Cave Hill.

Let it be, O Maaz, the ghazal is of Asian stock, your claim
to Jesus, your stigmata—they can't find, off the summit of Cave Hill.

URDU

اردو

دل ہی تو ہے نہ سنگ و خشت درد سے بھر نہ آئے کیوں
روئیں گے ہم ہزار بار کوئی ہمیں ستائے کیوں

دیر نہیں حرم نہیں در نہیں آستاں نہیں
بیٹھے ہیں رہ گزر پہ ہم غیر ہمیں اٹھائے کیوں

جب وہ جمال دلفروز صورت مہر نیم روز
آپ ہی ہو نظارہ سوز پردے میں منہ چھپائے کیوں

دشنۂ غمزہ جاں ستاں ناوک ناز بے پناہ
تیرا ہی عکس رخ سہی سامنے تیرے آئے کیوں

قید حیات و بند غم اصل میں دونوں ایک ہیں
موت سے پہلے آدمی غم سے نجات پائے کیوں

Merely a Heart

(dil hī to hai… by Mirza Ghalib)

Why should it not be full of pain,
merely a heart not a hard block of stone?
We shall cry ourselves a thousand times,
take jibes at us, why should anyone?

Not temple nor mosque, the Kaaba or a harem,
neither at a doorway nor a tomb or entrance.
We sit at common trodden pathways,
why remove us, O Unknown?

She, of the heart-warming beauty,
resplendent as the noon sun.
Herself a vision to blast all others,
why hide in a veil, all alone?

Piercing coquetry, bane of (my) life,
stinging endless arrows of pride.
Why would it come in front of you,
even if the image be your own?

Imprisoned by life or captive of grief,
both of these are one and the same.
Can man before death, in life itself,
ever find all his sorrows gone?

حسن اور اس پہ حسن ظن رہ گئی بوالہوس کی شرم
اپنے پہ اعتماد ہے غیر کو آزمائے کیوں

واں وہ غرور عز و ناز یاں یہ حجاب پاس وضع
راہ میں ہم ملیں کہاں بزم میں وہ بلائے کیوں

ہاں وہ نہیں خدا پرست جاؤ وہ بے وفا سہی
جس کو ہو دین و دل عزیز اس کی گلی میں جائے کیوں

غالبؔ خستہ کے بغیر کون سے کام بند ہیں
روئیے زار زار کیا کیجیے ہائے ہائے کیوں

-مرزا غالبؔ

Beauty and, with it, self-estimation,
saved my lusty rival from indiscretions.
There's confidence on the self,
why then a need to try that glutton?

There—she is arrogant and brimming with pride,
here—a humble humility about ourselves.
Where do we meet on the street?
Why'd she invite us to meets of her own?

Yes, I know she does not believe,
given she is unfaithful even.
Those who prize faith and fidelity,
to her lane—why'd they be shown?

Without the broken Ghalib, this world
would surely not come to a stop.
Why cry so bitterly then,
why make such a pitiful moan?

رہیے اب ایسی جگہ چل کر جہاں کوئی نہ ہو
ہم سخن کوئی نہ ہو اور ہم زباں کوئی نہ ہو

بے در و دیوار سا اک گھر بنایا چاہیے
کوئی ہمسایہ نہ ہو اور پاسباں کوئی نہ ہو

پڑیے گر بیمار تو کوئی نہ ہو تیماردار
اور اگر مر جائیے تو نوحہ خواں کوئی نہ ہو

—مرزا غالبؔ

Ghazalnāma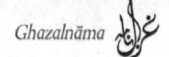

Let's Live in that Place

(rahiye ab aisī jagah… by Mirza Ghalib)

for Ammi

Let's live in that place where there's no one, let's go,
Where no one knows our tongue, there's no one to speak to.

We'd build a house without doors and walls,
Have no neighbours, watchmen forego.

In sickness no one to nurse us, enquire,
If we died, no one to mourn us, no!

ہزاروں خواہشیں ایسی کہ ہر خواہش پہ دم نکلے
بہت نکلے مرے ارمان لیکن پھر بھی کم نکلے

ڈرے کیوں میرا قاتل کیا رہے گا اس کی گردن پر
وہ خوں جو چشم تر سے عمر بھر یوں دم بدم نکلے

نکلنا خلد سے آدم کا سنتے آئے ہیں لیکن
بہت بے آبرو ہو کر ترے کوچے سے ہم نکلے

بھرم کھل جائے ظالم تیرے قامت کی درازی کا
اگر اس طرۂ پر پیچ و خم کا پیچ و خم نکلے

مگر لکھوائے کوئی اس کو خط تو ہم سے لکھوائے
ہوئی صبح اور گھر سے کان پر رکھ کر قلم نکلے

ہوئی اس دور میں منسوب مجھ سے بادہ آشامی
پھر آیا وہ زمانہ جو جہاں میں جام جم نکلے

Ghazalnāma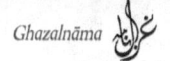

Thousands of Desires, Such

(hazāroñ khvāhisheñ aisī... by Mirza Ghalib)

Thousands of desires, such, that for every wish I'd die.
My many hopes came true, but many more did defy.

Should my killer be scared? Will it hang upon his neck?
—that blood which dropped lifelong from my ever brimming eye.

We'd always heard of Adam's exile from Eden, but,
When we left, we left your street so disgraced, all awry.

The myth would come undone, O Tyrant, of your growth in
stature, were the coils of your turban uncoiled, let fly.

If a letter to her be commissioned, we'll write that,
Come every morning, a quill on our ear we supply.

In that age was established, my habit for wine,
Once again the days for the jar of Jum to ply.[6]

Those who we hoped would harken to our woes,
Were more woebegone under the cruel sword's sway.

ہوئی جن سے توقع خستگی کی داد پانے کی
وہ ہم سے بھی زیادہ خستۂ تیغِ ستم نکلے

محبت میں نہیں ہے فرق جینے اور مرنے کا
اسی کو دیکھ کر جیتے ہیں جس کافر پہ دم نکلے

کہاں مے خانہ کا دروازہ غالبؔ اور کہاں واعظ
پر اتنا جانتے ہیں کل وہ جاتا تھا کہ ہم نکلے

—مرزا غالبؔ

Ghazalnāma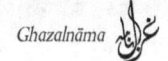

In love there is no difference in living and dying,
We live looking at our idol that takes our breath away.[7]

For God's sake do not remove the veil from the Kaaba,
O Tyrant! What if here too is my beloved idol's stay?[8]

Whither the way to the bar, Ghālib, and where the preacher,
Yet, we know that yesterday, thither he went, as we'd stray.

بازیچۂ اطفال ہے دنیا مرے آگے
ہوتا ہے شب و روز تماشا مرے آگے

اک کھیل ہے اورنگِ سلیماں مرے نزدیک
اک بات ہے اعجازِ مسیحا مرے آگے

جز نام نہیں صورتِ عالم مجھے منظور
جز وہم نہیں ہستیٔ اشیا مرے آگے

ہوتا ہے نہاں گرد میں صحرا مرے ہوتے
گھستا ہے جبیں خاک پہ دریا مرے آگے

مت پوچھ کہ کیا حال ہے میرا ترے پیچھے
تو دیکھ کہ کیا رنگ ہے تیرا مرے آگے

سچ کہتے ہو خودبین و خود آرا ہوں نہ کیوں ہوں
بیٹھا ہے بتِ آئینہ سیما مرے آگے

پھر دیکھیے اندازِ گل افشانیٔ گفتار
رکھ دے کوئی پیمانۂ صہبا مرے آگے

Child's Play

(bāzīcha-e-atfāl... by Mirza Ghalib)

A child's play is the world in front of me
Night and day, the tamasha is swirled in front of me

A game is the throne of Solomon to me,
The miracle of the Messiah too is told in front of me.

Not more than as a name do I accept this globe's mien,
A legend is the being of the world in front of me.

The desert's hidden with dust in my presence,
In dirt, the river's forehead is rubbed in front of me.

Don't ask of my condition in your absence,
You look at what colours you're pearled in, in front of me.

The doubts of hatred pass, I have passed through envy,
Why'd I say, don't let their name be called in front of me?

You speak truth that I am vain and arrogant too,
Behold there sits the silver-mirrored idol in front of me.

نفرت کا گماں گزرے ہے میں رشک سے گزرا
کیوں کر کہوں لو نام نہ ان کا مرے آگے

ایماں مجھے روکے ہے جو کھینچے ہے مجھے کفر
کعبہ مرے پیچھے ہے کلیسا مرے آگے

عاشق ہوں پہ معشوق فریبی ہے مرا کام
مجنوں کو برا کہتی ہے لیلیٰ مرے آگے

خوش ہوتے ہیں پر وصل میں یوں مر نہیں جاتے
آئی شب ہجراں کی تمنا مرے آگے

ہے موجزن اک قلزم خوں کاش یہی ہو
آتا ہے ابھی دیکھیے کیا کیا مرے آگے

گو ہاتھ کو جنبش نہیں آنکھوں میں تو دم ہے
رہنے دو ابھی ساغر و مینا مرے آگے

ہم پیشہ و ہم مشرب و ہم راز ہے میرا
غالبؔ کو برا کیوں کہو اچھا مرے آگے

—مرزا غالبؔ

Ghazalnāma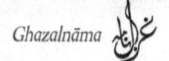

Look at the flow of words, my delivery's command,
If only you kept a glass of wine cuddled in front of me.

Faith stops me as sin draws me out,
The Kaaba is behind, a cathedral in front of me.

Since I am a lover, my profession is to cheat,
Laila calls Majnuñ a scoundrel in front of me.

We're happy at the union but we don't really die,
A hope for separation has rolled in front of me.

If only that tumultuous river of blood were this,
Let's see now what all is whirled in front of me.

If the hand has no reach, the eyes still see,
Let the bottle and glass be settled in front of me.

My colleague, my fellow drinker, my secret-keeper—he is,
Why call Ghalib bad?—he's of a better world, in front of me.

ہر ایک بات پہ کہتے ہو تم کہ تو کیا ہے
تمہیں کہو کہ یہ انداز گفتگو کیا ہے

نہ شعلہ میں یہ کرشمہ نہ برق میں یہ ادا
کوئی بتاؤ کہ وہ شوخ تند خو کیا ہے

یہ رشک ہے کہ وہ ہوتا ہے ہم سخن تم سے
وگرنہ خوف بد آموز عدو کیا ہے

چپک رہا ہے بدن پر لہو سے پیراہن
ہماری جیب کو اب حاجت رفو کیا ہے

جلا ہے جسم جہاں دل بھی جل گیا ہوگا
کریدتے ہو جو اب راکھ جستجو کیا ہے

رگوں میں دوڑتے پھرنے کے ہم نہیں قائل
جب آنکھ ہی سے نہ ٹپکا تو پھر لہو کیا ہے

وہ چیز جس کے لیے ہم کو ہو بہشت عزیز
سوائے بادۂ گلفام مشک بو کیا ہے

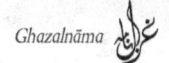

At Every Little Thing

(har ek bāt pe… by Mirza Ghalib)

At every little thing you say, 'Who art thou?'
Is this the way you talk to one, anyhow?

In flame not this miracle, in lightning not this art,
Tell me what's behind her bold, impulsive glow?

This jealousy is there that he confers with you
Else, what fear of the enemy's influence now?

With blood, my shirt sticks to the body,
What need of any darning does it allow?

Where the body's burnt, the heart would've too.
Raking the ashes, what do you seek now?

We are not convinced of simply running in the veins,
What blood that which from the eyes did not flow?

That thing for which we esteem Eden so high,
What is it but wine of the flower, musk of blossoms, mellow?

پیوں شراب اگر خم بھی دیکھ لوں دو چار
یہ شیشہ و قدح و کوزہ و سبو کیا ہے

رہی نہ طاقت گفتار اور اگر ہو بھی
تو کس امید پہ کہیے کہ آرزو کیا ہے

ہوا ہے شہ کا مصاحب پھرے ہے اتراتا
وگرنہ شہر میں غالبؔ کی آبرو کیا ہے

—مرزا غالبؔ

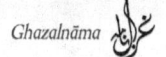

When it comes to drinks I see through a few barrels,
Why then in glass, goblet, or pitchers wallow?

Gone's the power of speech, and even if it
stayed, on what hope would I, my wishes, show?

Become the king's protégé, he struts about,
Else, what shall be Ghalib's fame in this town?

یہ نہ تھی ہماری قسمت کہ وصال یار ہوتا
اگر اور جیتے رہتے یہی انتظار ہوتا

ترے وعدے پر جیے ہم تو یہ جان جھوٹ جانا
کہ خوشی سے مر نہ جاتے اگر اعتبار ہوتا

تری نازکی سے جانا کہ بندھا تھا عہد بودا
کبھی تو نہ توڑ سکتا اگر استوار ہوتا

کوئی میرے دل سے پوچھے ترے تیر نیم کش کو
یہ خلش کہاں سے ہوتی جو جگر کے پار ہوتا

یہ کہاں کی دوستی ہے کہ بنے ہیں دوست ناصح
کوئی چارہ ساز ہوتا کوئی غم گسار ہوتا

رگ سنگ سے ٹپکتا وہ لہو کہ پھر نہ تھمتا
جسے غم سمجھ رہے ہو یہ اگر شرار ہوتا

It Wasn't Our Destiny

(ye na thī hamārī qismat… by Mirza Ghalib)

to Swarnim

It wasn't our destiny to be with our lover,
Had we lived anymore, the wait would've been longer!

I live by your promise, knowing it to be false,
Wouldn't I've died of joy, if I were a believer?

Through your caprice we learnt that the pledge was weak,
With such ease would it break if it were any stronger?

They should ask my heart, how your half-drawn arrows,
Could pierce it through, and where'd they get their power?

What friendship is this that friends become counselors?
There should've been a healer, a sympathizer!

Blood would pour unstoppably from the veins of marble,
What you believe to be grief may be scorching fire!

غم اگرچہ جاں گسل ہے پہ کہاں بچیں کہ دل ہے
غم عشق گر نہ ہوتا غم روزگار ہوتا

کہوں کس سے میں کہ کیا ہے شب غم بری بلا ہے
مجھے کیا برا تھا مرنا اگر ایک بار ہوتا

ہوئے مر کے ہم جو رسوا ہوئے کیوں نہ غرق دریا
نہ کبھی جنازہ اٹھتا نہ کہیں مزار ہوتا

اسے کون دیکھ سکتا کہ یگانہ ہے وہ یکتا
جو دوئی کی بو بھی ہوتی تو کہیں دو چار ہوتا

یہ مسائل تصوف یہ ترا بیان غالبؔ
تجھے ہم ولی سمجھتے جو نہ بادہ خوار ہوتا

-مرزا غالبؔ

Ghazalnāma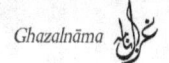

If this torment's heart-breaking, where'd we go hiding?
If it weren't the pain of love, it'd be of our career.

To whom do I complain, of this sad night's refrain?
Death wouldn't be too bad, if only once it were.

This dishonour on death, why didn't we drown instead?
There would've been no tomb, there would've been no bier.

Who can see Him? He is One, the Monad. Were there
any duality, our four eyes would pair.

These matters of mystic thought, these renderings of yours,
Ghalib, we'd call you a saint, were you not a drinker.

کوئی امید بر نہیں آتی
کوئی صورت نظر نہیں آتی

موت کا ایک دن معیّن ہے
نیند کیوں رات بھر نہیں آتی

آگے آتی تھی حال دل پہ ہنسی
اب کسی بات پر نہیں آتی

جانتا ہوں ثواب طاعت و زہد
پر طبیعت ادھر نہیں آتی

ہے کچھ ایسی ہی بات جو چپ ہوں
ورنہ کیا بات کر نہیں آتی

کیوں نہ چیخوں کہ یاد کرتے ہیں
میری آواز گر نہیں آتی

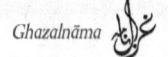

Not a Wish Comes to Fruition

(koi ummīd bar nahiñ ātī… by Mirza Ghalib)

Not a wish comes to fruition.
I can see no conclusion.

The day for death is a given,
Then why can't I sleep this season?

I could laugh at myself once,
Now no humour, just remission.

I know the rewards for faith, still,
That is not my predilection.

There is a reason I am quiet now,
Else I'm eloquent of conversation.

Why should I not shout in remembrance?
Inaudible is my voice of reason.

داغ دل گر نظر نہیں آتا
بو بھی اے چارہ گر نہیں آتی

ہم وہاں ہیں جہاں سے ہم کو بھی
کچھ ہماری خبر نہیں آتی

مرتے ہیں آرزو میں مرنے کی
موت آتی ہے پر نہیں آتی

کعبہ کس منہ سے جاؤ گے غالبؔ
شرم تم کو مگر نہیں آتی

-مرزا غالبؔ

If the wounds of my heart are not visible,
There's no stench either, O Physician.

We are there where to us, even,
Comes no news of our condition.

We die in the hope of dying (for love),
Death waits, with its repetition.

How will you show your face at the Kaaba, Ghalib?
You know no shame, only humiliation.

نہ تھا کچھ تو خدا تھا کچھ نہ ہوتا تو خدا ہوتا
ڈبویا مجھ کو ہونے نے نہ ہوتا میں تو کیا ہوتا

ہوا جب غم سے یوں بے حس تو غم کیا سر کے کٹنے کا
نہ ہوتا گر جدا تن سے تو زانو پر دھرا ہوتا

ہوئی مدت کہ غالبؔ مر گیا پر یاد آتا ہے
وہ ہر اک بات پر کہنا کہ یوں ہوتا تو کیا ہوتا

—مرزا غالبؔ

Being

(na thā kuch to k͟hudā tha… by Mirza Ghalib)

When there was nothing, was God, if there were nothing,
 would be God,
My being defeated me, had I not been, what would've been?

When I've grown blasé of grief then what grief over my beheading?
Had it not been severed from my body, on the knees—
 it would've been.

It's been an age that he died, but the memory of Ghalib lives,
At every little thing, his saying: what would be if this had been?

رقیب سے

آ کہ وابستہ ہیں اس حسن کی یادیں تجھ سے
جس نے اس دل کو پری خانہ بنا رکھا تھا
جس کی الفت میں بھلا رکھی تھی دنیا ہم نے
دہر کو دہر کا افسانہ بنا رکھا تھا

آشنا ہیں ترے قدموں سے وہ راہیں جن پر
اس کی مدہوش جوانی نے عنایت کی ہے
کارواں گزرے ہیں جن سے اسی رعنائی کے
جس کی ان آنکھوں نے بے سود عبادت کی ہے

تجھ سے کھیلی ہیں وہ محبوب ہوائیں جن میں
اس کے ملبوس کی افسردہ مہک باقی ہے
تجھ پہ برسا ہے اسی بام سے مہتاب کا نور
جس میں بیتی ہوئی راتوں کی کسک باقی ہے

تو نے دیکھی ہے وہ پیشانی وہ رخسار وہ ہونٹ
زندگی جن کے تصوّر میں لٹا دی ہم نے
تجھ پہ اٹھی ہیں وہ کھوئی ہوئی ساحر آنکھیں
تجھ کو معلوم ہے کیوں عمر گنوا دی ہم نے

Ghazalnāma

To the Rival

(raqib se… by Faiz Ahmed Faiz)

for Basit

Come, for the memories of beauty are linked to you,
That had converted the heart into a fairy-house,
In whose love we had forgotten the world,
And had turned time and the world into their tales.

Those lanes are acquainted with your steps,
That were favoured by her intoxicated youth,
Where caravans have passed of that very beauty,
Which these eyes had worshipped without a thought for gains.

Those loving winds have played with you,
That carry the melancholic smell of her garb,
On you too showered the splendour of that moon over the terrace,
Which carries the pain of those nights that are gone.

You have seen that brow, those rosy cheeks, those lips,
Contemplating which, we spent our lives,
Those conjuring eyes were raised to you too,
You know why we have lost an age.

ہم پہ مشترکہ ہیں احسان غم الفت کے
اتنے احسان کہ گنواؤں تو گنوا نہ سکوں
ہم نے اس عشق میں کیا کھویا ہے کیا سیکھا ہے
جز ترے اور کو سمجھاؤں تو سمجھا نہ سکوں

عاجزی سیکھی غریبوں کی حمایت سیکھی
یاس و حرماں کے دکھ درد کے معنی سیکھے
زیر دستوں کے مصائب کو سمجھنا سیکھا
سرد آہوں کے رخ زرد کے معنی سیکھے

جب کہیں بیٹھ کے روتے ہیں وہ بیکس جن کے
اشک آنکھوں میں بلکتے ہوئے سو جاتے ہیں
نا توانوں کے نوالوں پہ جھپٹتے ہیں عقاب
بازو تولے ہوئے منڈلاتے ہوئے آتے ہیں

جب کبھی بکتا ہے بازار میں مزدور کا گوشت
شاہراہوں پہ غریبوں کا لہو بہتا ہے
آگ سی سینے میں رہ رہ کے ابلتی ہے نہ پوچھ
اپنے دل پر مجھے قابو ہی نہیں رہتا ہے

-فیض احمد فیض-

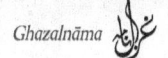

We are joined in the favours bestowed by the sorrows
of love, so many favours that I couldn't count,
What we have lost and what we have learnt in love,
but for you, to whom do I explain this, and how?

Learnt humility, empathy with the poor, we learnt,
The meanings of hopelessness, despair, grief and pain,
We learned to understand the miseries of the servant,
Made sense of the pale faces of the cold sighs.

When those helpless sit and cry somewhere, whose
tears dry up in their eyes as they weep,
The falcons come in flocks flexing their muscles
and pounce on the morsels of the weak.

Whenever the worker's flesh is sold in the bazaar,
The blood of the poor flows on the high roads,
A fire rages in my chest, don't ask me of it,
I retain no control over my heart!

یاد

دشت تنہائی میں اے جان جہاں لرزاں ہیں
تیری آواز کے سائے ترے ہونٹوں کے سراب
دشت تنہائی میں دوری کے خس و خاک تلے
کھل رہے ہیں ترے پہلو کے سمن اور گلاب

اٹھ رہی ہے کہیں قربت سے تری سانس کی آنچ
اپنی خوشبو میں سلگتی ہوئی مدھم مدھم
دور افق پار چمکتی ہوئی قطرہ قطرہ
گر رہی ہے تری دل دار نظر کی شبنم

اس قدر پیار سے اے جان جہاں رکھا ہے
دل کے رخسار پہ اس وقت تری یاد نے ہاتھ
یوں گماں ہوتا ہے گرچہ ہے ابھی صبح فراق
ڈھل گیا ہجر کا دن آ بھی گئی وصل کی رات

—فیض احمد فیض

Remembrance

(yaad by Faiz Ahmed Faiz)

to Nabanita Kanungo

In the desert of loneliness, quiver
the shadows of your voice, my beloved, and your lips' mirage.
In the desert of loneliness, under swathes of dust and ash,
bloom the jasmines and the roses after your heart.

The warmth of your breath rises in the vicinity,
smouldering slowly in its own fragrance.
In the distance of the horizon, falling drop by drop,
glistens the dew from your generous glance.

With such love, my beloved, has your memory,
today, touched the flanks of my heart,
that even if this is a morning apart,
the day of rift seems at an end, comes the night of our match.

کافی

ہوری کھیلوں گی، کہہ بسم اللہ
نام نبی کی رتن چڑھی بوند پڑی اللہ اللہ
رنگ رنگیلی، اوہی کھلاوے
جس سیکھی ہو فنا فی اللہ
اَلَسْتُ بِرَبِّکُمْ — پریتم بولے
سب سکھیاں نے گھونگھٹ کھولے
قَالُوا بَلٰی — یوں ہی کر بولے —
لَا اِلٰہَ اِلَّا اللّٰہ
ہوری کھیلوں گی، کہہ بسم اللہ

— بلّے شاہ

Holi

(kaafi, which is attributed to Bulleh Shah)

I will play Holi beginning in the name of the Lord,
saying bismillah.

Cast like a gem in the name of the prophet,
Each drop falls with the beat of Al-lah, Al-lah,
Only he may play with these colourful dyes,
Who has learnt to lose himself in Allah.

'Am I not your lord?' asked the Lover,
And all maids lifted their veils,
'Everyone said, yes!' and repeated:
'There is only one God.'

I will play Holi beginning in the name of the Lord,
saying bismillah.

رنگ

آج رنگ ہے ری ماں رنگ ہے ری

مورے محبوب کے گھر رنگ ہے ری

سجن ملاورا مورے آنگن کو

آج رنگ ہے ری ماں رنگ ہے ری

موہے پیر پایو—نظام الدین اولیاء

نظام الدین اولیاء— موہے پیر پایو

دیس بدیس میں ڈھونڈھ پھری ہوں

تورا رنگ من بھایو نظام الدین

آج رنگ ہے ری ماں رنگ ہے ری

جگ اجیارو جگت اجیارو

میں نے ایسو رنگ اور نہیں دیکھی ری

میں تو جب دیکھوں مورے سنگ ہے ری ماں

میں تو جب دیکھوں مورے سنگ ہے ری ماں

آج رنگ ہے ری ماں رنگ ہے ری

—امیر خسرو

Colour

(rang, which is attributed to Amir Khusrau)

to Dibyajyoti

There's colour today, O Mother, there's a glow today,
In my beloved's home there's new colour today.
I've met my beloved, I've found him,
In my own yard,
It's radiant today!
There's colour today, O Mother, there's a glow today.

I've discovered my saint, Nizamuddin Aulia,
Nizamuddin Aulia, he is my saint!
I have travelled far and wide, here and abroad,
Searching,
It's your person, your glow that's tinged my heart.
You've lit up the world, the universe is lit,
Never have I seen such splendour,
Whenever I look around, he's there with me.
There's colour today, O Mother, there's a glow today.

یا مجھے افسر شاہانہ بنایا ہوتا
یا مرا تاج گدایانہ بنایا ہوتا

اپنا دیوانہ بنایا مجھے ہوتا تو نے
کیوں خرد مند بنایا نہ بنایا ہوتا

خاکساری کے لیے گرچہ بنایا تھا مجھے
کاش خاک در جانانہ بنایا ہوتا

نشۂ عشق کا گر ظرف دیا تھا مجھ کو
عمر کا تنگ نہ پیمانہ بنایا ہوتا

دل صد چاک بنایا تو بلا سے لیکن
زلف مشکیں کا ترے شانہ بنایا ہوتا

صوفیوں کے جو نہ تھا لائق صحبت تو مجھے
قابل جلسۂ رندانہ بنایا ہوتا

تھا جلانا ہی اگر دوریٔ ساقی سے مجھے
تو چراغ در مے خانہ بنایا ہوتا

The Master of Royals

(yā mujhe afsar-e-shāhāna… by Bahadur Shah Zafar)

I wish you had made me the master of royals,
Or made my crown the bowl for alms and betrayals.

You should have made me mad, crazy only for you,
Why did you make me wise, capable of denials?

You made me poor, fit only for sifting through dust,
And I wish the dust of her feet were my trials.

If you made me intoxicated with love,
Why did you make the measure of life small vials?

A wretched heart torn a hundred times over lives,
To be the shoulder to rest her hair is my desire.

If I were not worthy to be with the Sufis,
Could have been good for the company of drunks, defiant?

If you wished to burn me by parting from the pourer,
Should have made me the lamp of the tavern's foyer.

شعلۂ حسن چمن میں نہ دکھایا اس نے
ورنہ بلبل کو بھی پروانہ بنایا ہوتا

روز معمورۂ دنیا میں خرابی ہے ظفرؔ
ایسی بستی کو تو ویرانہ بنایا ہوتا

—بہادر شاہ ظفرؔ

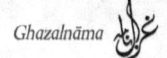

The fire of beauty was not unveiled in the garden,
Or the bulbul too would have been made a moth on fire.

This incessant world is a vile place, O Zafar,
Its cities should have been desolate and dire.

جگر کے ٹکڑے ہوئے جل کے دل کباب ہوا
یہ عشق جان کو میرے کوئی عذاب ہوا

کیا جو قتل مجھے تم نے خوب کام کیا
کہ میں عذاب سے چھوٹا تمہیں ثواب ہوا

کبھی تو شیفتہ اس نے کہا کبھی شیدا
غرض کہ روز نیا اک مجھے خطاب ہوا

پیوں نہ رشک سے خوں کیونکہ دم بہ دم اپنا
کہ ساتھ غیر کے وہ آج ہم شراب ہوا

تمہارے لب کے لب جام نے لیے بوسے
لب اپنے کاٹا کیا میں نہ کامیاب ہوا

گلی گلی تری خاطر پھرا بہ چشم پر آب
لگا کے تجھ سے دل اپنا بہت خراب ہوا

Ghazalnāma

The Heart is Asunder

(jigar ke TukṚe hue… by Bahadur Shah Zafar)

The heart is asunder, singed to a kebab,
This love has been the disaster of my life.

My murder rests good on you, don't worry,
You have found grace, I am away from strife.

'Enamoured' one day, 'mad' on another,
Each day I was given new names, new life.

Why should I not drink my blood in envy?
When today, with my rival they wine.

The goblet's lips kissed yours in ecstasy,
My victory was to bite into mine.

For you, I wandered streets with tearful eyes,
Setting my heart on you was misery.

تری گلی میں بہائے پھرے ہے سیلِ سرشک
ہمارا کاسۂ سر کیا ہوا حباب ہوا

جواب خط کے نہ لکھنے سے یہ ہوا معلوم
کہ آج سے ہمیں اے نامہ بر جواب ہوا

منگائی تھی تری تصویر دل کی تسکیں کو
مجھے تو دیکھتے ہی اور اضطراب ہوا

ستم تمہارے بہت اور دن حساب کا ایک
مجھے ہے سوچ یہ ہی کس طرح حساب ہوا

ظفرؔ بدل کے ردیف اور تو غزل وہ سنا
کہ جس کا تجھ سے ہر اک شعر انتخاب ہوا

—بہادر شاہ ظفرؔ

Ghazalnāma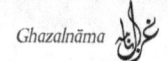

We have washed your street with a storm of tears,
Our begging bowl of a cap is now empty.

Without replies now, this is what we found,
That the messenger is our sole reply.

Had asked for your picture to console my heart,
Looking at it I am more uneasy.

Your tyranny—boundless, day of reck'ning—one,
I wonder how the account is compiled.

Zafar, change the refrain, recite that ghazal,
Of which each verse is your picked poetry.

میں ہوں عاصی کہ پر خطا کچھ ہوں
تیرا بندہ ہوں اے خدا کچھ ہوں

جزو و کل کو نہیں سمجھتا میں
دل میں تھوڑا سا جانتا کچھ ہوں

تجھ سے الفت نباہتا ہوں میں
با وفا ہوں کہ بے وفا کچھ ہوں

جب سے ناآشنا ہوں میں سب سے
تب کہیں اس سے آشنا کچھ ہوں

نشہ عشق لے اڑا ہے مجھے
اب مزے میں اڑا رہا کچھ ہوں

خواب میرا ہے عین بیداری
میں تو اس میں بھی دیکھتا کچھ ہوں

گرچہ کچھ بھی نہیں ہوں میں لیکن
اس پہ بھی کچھ نہ پوچھو کیا کچھ ہوں

Somewhat

(maiñ huuñ aasī ki pur-ḳhatā... by Bahadur Shah Zafar)

I am the sinner's fault, somewhat,
Your devotee, O God, somewhat.

I do not understand whole or part,
In my heart, I know not all, somewhat.

I remain loyal to you,
Faithful I am, faithless—somewhat.

Since I do not meet any other,
With him I have communion—somewhat.

The intoxication of love has given me flight,
In bliss, I fly with faith, somewhat.

My dreams lie in wakefulness,
I see better visions there, somewhat.

I may not be anyone, yet,
Don't ask—I am what I am—somewhat.

سمجھے وہ اپنا خاکسار مجھے
خاک رہ ہوں کہ خاک پا کچھ ہوں

چشم الطاف فخر دیں سے ہوں
اے ظفرؔ کچھ سے ہو گیا کچھ ہوں

-بہادر شاہ ظفرؔ

Ghazalnāma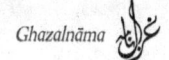

Let them think me their humble servant,
I am the dust of the road, of the feet—somewhat.

I have got the blessed eye of faith,
O Zafar, from something I have moved to somewhat.

گاندھی ہو یا غالب ہو

گاندھی ہو یا غالب ہو
ختم ہوا دونوں کا جشن
آؤ انہیں اب کر دیں دفن
ختم کرو تہذیب کی بات   بند کرو کلچر کا شور
ستیہ اہنسا سب بکواس   ہم بھی قاتل تم بھی چور
ختم ہوا دونوں کا جشن
آؤ انہیں اب کر دیں دفن
وہ بستی وہ گاؤں ہی کیا   جس میں ہریجن ہو آزاد
وہ قصبہ وہ شہر ہی کیا   جو نہ بنے احمد آباد
ختم ہوا دونوں کا جشن
آؤ انہیں اب کر دیں دفن

Be it Gandhi, Be it Ghalib[9]

(Gandhi ho ya Ghalib ho by Sahir Ludhianvi)

to Arunava Sinha

Be it Gandhi, be it Ghalib,
    The celebrations for both are at an end,
    Come, let's bury both of them.

Let's stop talking civilization,
Let's shut down all cultural noise.

Truth, Ahimsa are all nonsense,
You're a murderer, I'm the robber!

    The celebrations for both are at an end,
    Come, let's bury both of them.

What settlement, what village is that,
Where the Harijan is free?

What district, which city is it,
That will not an Ahmedabad[10] be?

    The celebrations for both are at an end,
    Come, let's bury both of them.

گاندھی ہو یا غالب ہو   دونوں کا کیا کام یہاں
اب کے برس بھی قتل ہوئی   ایک کی شِکشا اک کی زباں
ختم ہوا دونوں کا جشن
آؤ انہیں اب کر دیں دفن

—ساحر لدھیانوی

Ghazalnāma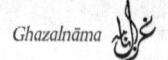

Be it Gandhi, be it Ghalib,
Of what use are both today?

This year too, they have killed—
The teachings of one, the other's tongue.

    The celebrations for both are at an end,
    Come, let's bury both of them.

DELHI AGAIN

پھر دہلی

Ghazalnāma

Air Black

to Sridala Swami and the winter of 2014–15

She says yesterday's faded-denim sky
of many washes
brought down leaves that
were not choked with dust.

My sky today was a crumpled khakhi
with dirt like the Sirocco's,
but in still air, without the strong breeze,
only the dust.

Her dust free leaves flew around,
settled on the ground, were
picked up again,
by the wind, and made
patterns, did rounds.

No current moves the cloud
settled over our heads here.
The leaf my nephew picks and navigates
around with, playing with it like a plane
in his hand, will not lose that
film
of dust,
that's settled!

Delhi is one thick haze
of that cheap opium den,
where everyone's an addict
of toxic scum.

Muslimah

a poem in six voices

I

The Saudi in the Audi

Yeah, you're right, I drove that Audi,
in prison, I am, I am the woman of Saudi!

Yeah, read this right,
and hold on tight,
as I make some way,
for my sistah's fight.[11]

II

The Hijab Examination

On the third of May,
in great dismay,
I went to attest
for the sake of protest,
to my own shame,
I sat the pre-med test.

To appear for an exam,
I had to undergo the sham
of having to reveal,
to forcibly peal,

my second skin,
in front of the non-kin.

A turbaned man,
also sat the exam.
His beard and headgear,
had not my scarf's smear.

III

The Researcher from Syria

I heard her in Newcastle,
at a conference
on practising
the PoCo way.

Her work, on
women's health
in Aleppo,
Syria.
The data she'd collected, so
painstakingly,
was from earlier times of peace.

Now, absolutely
meaningless.
Tending more to a cipher each day.

As she presented it,
devoid of referent,

she could not hold back her tears,
which flowed freely to express
her grief for the primeval.

Aleppo, now rubble, and desolate,
had, till recently, been
the world's oldest,
inhabited city.

It filled her voice, that dust, it choked her throat.

A medical anthropologist,
the numbers in her hands, they used to be women,
now meaningless.

The numbers in her hand, they used to be women,
people, who were no more.
They'd returned to that dirt from which they came.
Made of flesh, woman like man, man like child, all gone back
to the earth, their mother.

IV

Mothers of Gaza

In Gaza there are no sons.
In Gaza we want daughters.
In Gaza let's not procreate.
In Gaza they've an expiry date.

V

Call to Mrs Rehman

Hello, Mrs Rehman!
What date is Eid this time?
We're all so missing the *biryani* from last year!
And the *kebabs*, just to die for!
And Mr S, here, just swears by your *shir*!
You know I tried your *qorma* recipe?
But it's just not the same!
I can't ever get it right!

VI

Right in the Face

Oh yes, I got it right in the face,
that bullet that sought to end an idea.
But all the love out there made me stronger,
all fears and 'my hopelessness died on that day'.[12]
I fly now, I educate, I teach girls, to blow the world away.

Ghazalnāma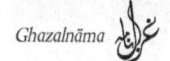

To Michelangelo and Aditi Rao

The God and the father,
the father and the God,
that reaching hand,
the loosened grasp.

'Tomorrow we too
will find ways
to let each other down.'

We shall not be made into frescoes,
it won't amount to anything profound,
just promises to be made,
and broken,
forays, and turnarounds.

In His Heart

to Divya

Love at first sight, a thunderclap in his heart.
Still never, her, could he trap in his heart.

She was the joy of dance, the tinkle of glass,
She cut too like a shard, how strap in his heart?

Madness and tears; like fish without water,
Identitarian souls that flap in his heart.

Bad manners, daily squabbles, humiliations,
The family's jibes, like a slap in his heart.

It's turned to stone now, so pin down some love,
And squeeze in some life through the gap in his heart.

The lost sister—a wound, it needs sutures,
Find some salve and put a wrap in his heart.

Bottled up emotions and stifled grief; let
ululations refill the sap in his heart.

Insomniac ramblings, poetry's limitations,
May the eternal Nyx choose to nap in his heart.

Leave those lanes that bind you and travel abroad—
A new spring and a new clap in his heart.

Cold streets of isolation, warm cups of wine,
As another string would snap in his heart.

Maaz thought he would live happily in Europe,
Did he know he had Delhi's map in his heart?

Haiku I

She sends me an X,
Every night on chat. On it's
Edge, I'll cut a lip.

Haiku II

On murmurations
Of starlings, send me your love.
The email's old school.

Stardust

> *'Never was a man treated as a mind.*
> *As a glorious thing made up of stardust.'*
>
> —Suicide Note of Rohith Vemula

One grew up familiar in India with the magazine of Stardust,
Then the word acquired new meaning, the real sheen of stardust.

It will be the aura of lady-killer Khans no more,
Bhim's descendants call for the whole tureen of stardust.

The bold and reckless, the spotless fear this dirt,
They wish to stifle the power foreseen of stardust.

All of us made up of this substance, some abuse it
more than others, the in-between of stardust.

The Goths took refuge in Antilia, it's a monstrosity now
in the city of slums, the obscene of stardust.

Some stardust is fed by foie gras, others try and fail
to sell their kidneys, the untouched, unseen of stardust.

Blood is up for spoils, but will it ever boil?
When a light dies, will we careen off stardust?

You inherited it reduced to kitsch, gossip of films, Maaz,
Rohith reclaimed your make-up, made up, pristine, of stardust.

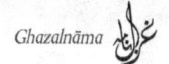

A Shriek About Kashmir, July 2016

to Abir Bazaz, Javaid Iqbal Bhat, Hamzah, and all my Kashmiri brothers.

How do I see, think, dream, or speak about Kashmir?
One more ghazal shall I tweak about Kashmir?

Another bloody summer looms over the Dal,
Wani's died and been deified this week, about Kashmir.

Vani is also voice in Hindi and Sanskrit,
There's a roar now not a creak about Kashmir.

Thirty killed or martyred in only three days,
What vengeance is this that we seek about Kashmir?

Pandits were driven out, and Muslims are curfewed in,
Of raw flesh and fury—a reek about Kashmir.

A green land of saffron, of rishis and shairs,
What is Indian, what is unique about Kashmir?

Courting bullets on streets are those sons of the soil,
Swaraj, their birthright, kindles the pique about Kashmir.

A mighty pretty valley, its people's mighty will,
What is strong, and what is weak about Kashmir?

Relentless calls for Azadi, will it ever come?
Is there debate, any critique about Kashmir?

A handsome boy died, which a nation defied,
Beauty, power, what is the mystique about Kashmir?

Here is no place for a *maqta* this time, Maaz,
Humiliation, pain wreak (havoc) about Kashmir.

This summer, snows have melted into tears of rage,
Burhan's voice has become a shriek about Kashmir.

Let's War, Said He

to e. e. cummings

Let's war, said he,
Oh, come on, said he,
You're my dratted enemy,
But we can live peaceably.

Let's war said he,
We're nuclear, said he,
And terrorists, said he,
But you shot first, said he.

You kill civilians, said he,
We kill traitors, said he,
You are fascists, said he,
We're nationalists, said he.

Let's do war, said he,
Oh yes, let's see,
Aren't you afraid?—said he,
We aren't friendless, said he.

I have big guns, said he,
We have balls, said he,
Remember that war?—said he,
Remember those two?—said he.

We have a massive army!
We're passionate, said he.
So belligerent, are we?
Not a step behind, you see.

Let's war, said he,
Bring it on, said he,
Call your man, said he,
He's already on, said he.

Well, what's the wait, said he?
Your move, said he,
It's yours, said he,
Didn't you want it more?—said he.

. . .

We can't really war, can we?
Not on each other, I don't see.
But at war, we must be!
Yes, but on whom can it be?

There are many, don't you see?
Ah yes, there are many, I see.
Look, there is she,
Yes, yes, there is she.

The Frogs in Her Dreams

to Andrew Rooney

She couldn't know if those were frogs in her dreams,
The shadows that haunt her, the dogs in her dreams.

She counts sheep to sleep, or skyfuls of scars,
Death keeps time, maintains her logs in her dreams.

Sisyphus ran down to fetch his burden
in joy. Absurd, she still slogs in her dreams.

She loved him deeply, that shit of a cheat,
Yet some prime real estate he hogs in her dreams.

A weedy genre—this English ghazal,
Maaz, are you cloning the fogs in her dreams?

Amaltas–Monsoon

*to Anannya Dasgupta and Uttaran Das Gupta, and
for Suchismita*

I

As crusts over hearts may bake in this season of amaltas,
Our parched souls, if florid, ache in this season of amaltas.

> Then unbearable yellow blooms are drenched by the monsoon,
> The thirst of Qais's solitude is quenched by the monsoon.

In that blinding yellow haze, what, did we not rake in those
inflamed passions, the sun's make, in this season of amaltas?

> Did the rain then dissipate what desire did create?
> Did water douse raging fires, belched by the monsoon?

Delhi's very own harvest, for the soaked lover, what rest?
Crackdowns, protests; what'll he take in this season of amaltas?

> It's thunder, lightning; will the revolution be frightening?
> Or will all beauty, romance now be wrenched by the monsoon?

You're out to find roses at the time of laburnums, Maaz,
They will know you're a fake, in this season of amaltas.

> But think of it again, Maaz, could this be your final stance?
> The thick fleece of yellow fur may be flenched by the monsoon.

II

In summer:

As crusts over hearts may bake in this season of amaltas,
Our parched souls, if florid, ache in this season of amaltas.

In that blinding yellow haze, what, did we not rake in those
inflamed passions, the sun's make, in this season of amaltas?

Delhi's very own harvest, for the soaked lover, what rest?
Crackdowns, protests; what'll he take in this season of amaltas?

You're out to find roses at the time of laburnums, Maaz,
They will know you're a fake, in this season of amaltas.

And then come the rains:

When unbearable yellow blooms are drenched by the monsoon,
The thirst of Qais's solitude is quenched by the monsoon.

Did the rain then dissipate what desire did create?
Did water douse raging fires, belched by the monsoon?

It's thunder, lightning; will the revolution be frightening?
Or will all beauty, romance now be wrenched by the monsoon?

But think of it again, Maaz, could this be your final stance?
The thick fleece of yellow fur may be flenched by the monsoon.

Agra, 1948

> *I want to tell them frankly that mere declarations of loyalty to the Indian Union will not help them at this critical juncture. They must give practical proof of their declarations.*
> *—You Cannot Ride Two Horses*
> *(Speech by Sardar Patel on 6 January 1948, in Lucknow)*

I

Why did you sell your house now, O Khadim?
As hereditary guard of the Taj Mahal, must you not be prim
and proper, when for Pakistan has left,
all your family, most of your kin?

II

There are four reasons for the sale, Sahib:
I owed debts, and I have daughters to be married,
The refugees living in my house misused it,
My sons have gone, I need money, for when I die, to be buried.

III

Tch, tch, I am sorry, I am not convinced,
Why now? Never before you felt pinched?
Go fetch positive proof of your faith, in a month,
else lose your job, we believe in your guilt.

Ghazalnāma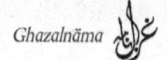

IV

Here, Sir, I have brought back from Lahore,
my two daughters, orphaned grandchildren—four.
The rest won't come, they fear their old neighbours,
Please don't fire me, by God, I could do no more.

(Based on real events)[13]

Lessons in World Geography

The Indian adolescent was now learning the geography of his country through the history of murder.
                              —Khushwant Singh, c. late 1960s.

I

I was five when 9/11 happened,
A plane flew into a tower, then one more
into another, I asked mother if it were
a video game, she said, no, that's the Big Apple.

II

By six I knew Kabul, Kandahar, Herat,
and Bamyan, and closer to home Godhra, Shopian,
our Amdavad, although these I heard more than
saw (mother won't allow me to watch TV), still
I could locate them all on the map.

III

By seven opened a whole new world:
Basra, Najaf, Baghdad, Mosul.
An evil man was being hunted here
by the G. I. Joes, he was pinned like a rat.

IV

Over time our TV kept telling me,
Of Syria, Sudan, Gaza, and the Somali,
Today I am twenty-one and have a degree,
(Mosul's just been redeemed),
but I did not need one in geography.

The Law

An Ode to Habib Jalib

The law that constricts a woman to her home,
turns her into a paid-for whore,
prevents man from loving men,
and obstructs their dietary regimen,

such a law, on this murky dawn,
I cannot accept.

Where my speech carries more hate
than that of the worst, and won't abate
come what I do, as prisons are filled
with under-trial lovers, if not killed,

such a law, on this murky dawn,
I cannot accept.

You say the kites are in flight again,
it is spring, the cold reign of the dark at an end,
you say that we have prospered beyond count
even as village trees are laden, with more than just fruit.

such a lie, on this murky dawn,
I won't accept.

Ghazalnāma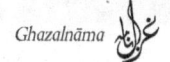

I won't say that I am not scared of the prison,
for it is no longer run by a power that would listen
to reason, or believe in any dignity,
but knows naked power, all cruelty,

such a law, on this murky dawn,
I won't accept.

You have plundered us for hundreds of years,
put us in systems of margins and gushing tears,
where the mighty and many rule the weak and few,
this evacuation of body and mind, to curfew,

on this murky dawn, with its law,
I won't accept.

Champa

White petals
with yellow hints
in your hair, you have
become the umbrella tree.

Come, shade me,
from the rain of a
people's pain, come
share your slow ecstasy,
frangipani.

Ghazalnāma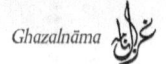

Night and Day

For Kunal

> *mat puuchh ke kya haal hai mera tere piichhe...*
> —Mirza Ghalib

My lover left for fairer shores of snow, where it is night, here day,
Not a peep, no tweet, no letter-spoor, as I miss (him), night and day.

He is a master actor, could feign fidelity, but his charm's
disaffection, a quietude, isolation to caress night and day.

Yet, he could be Tigger-hyper, a pixie-Pan, or a satyr,
He'd enchant whole continents; no heart enough—his (are)
    night and day.

I believe he's my brother, not just lighter but kinder; for he
sat me, the terrorist, at his table with a lie of bliss, night and day.

Was he real or a ghoul, the wisest or a tool, gone with winter
to the moon, to help steer multipolar earth, redress night and day?

He's writing our history of violence, hence this silence, or why wouldn't
he write to me, Maaz, paeans of peace and love, and bless night and day?

I just crossed the seas, to slay the beast of yearning, he was nowhere to be found, yet to come around, unleash the word to suppress night and day.

 *Ghazalnāma*

Caravans of Love

after Harsh Mander and Suchismita

To breathe of your breath, not to die in love.
Rebellion must be all, defy in love.

Sameness is the bane of this life,
To difference I go, to test and try in love.

What are my limits? The test of your patience.
I can wage holy wars, why cry in love?

Ethics of the other, all pleasures for myself,
Accept, commit, care, comply in love.

To see this world with not two but four eyes,
When revelation's all your sky in love.

The faults of the moon, the heat of the stars,
Forget desire, dream to fly in love.

Lead caravans of love, touch people's misery,
Love's bonds, love's politics—love, love, love, love—
Go on, forget your I in love.

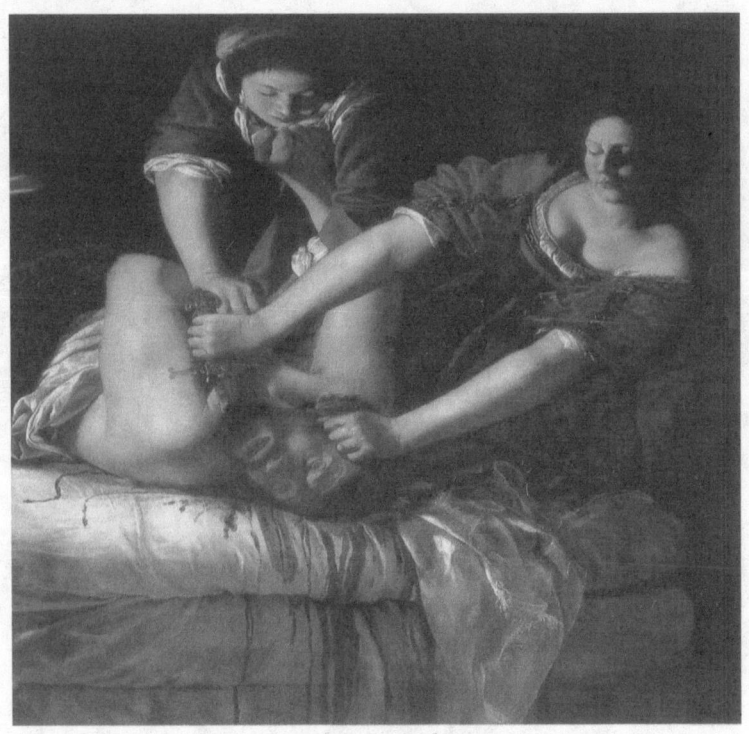

'Judith slaying Holofernes' painting by Artemisia Gentileschi

Ghazal after Adrienne Rich

for Yasodhara

He loved my spirit, my mind, my body, he proposed,
Then he became conservative.

We lived a world apart, a river of fire spread between us,
To think of his warmth now makes me shudder.

I love films, he often slept during them,
I wonder how I looked in his dreams.

Sleep is the luxury denied to the pauper,
I weave my winks into the choker of our lies.

Edna Millay forgot the lips she'd kissed,[14]
Gentileschi beheaded the Tassies of her life.[15]

ENDNOTES

1. Ballimaran is a locality in Chandni Chowk, Delhi, India, where the haveli of the poet, Ghalib, stands even today.
2. *'ye na thi hamāri qismat ke visāl-e-yār hotā'*.
3. The night when Muhammad is believed to have travelled to the heavens and back.
4. Ablutions before *salāt*.
5. This poem owes its title to the title of an anthology of Caribbean literature.
6. The mythical cup of Jamshed of Persia meant for divination. The original *jaam-e-jum* has an alliteration that is sought to be recreated here.
7. I have translated *kāfir* as idol here, though *kāfir* would literally translate as idolater or pagan, which is how it is often rendered in translations of this ghazal. However, it is the beloved here who is referred as *kāfir* not because s/he is a non-believer but because s/he leads the narrator towards intense devotion and worship of herself, which is equal to *shirk* or polytheism in Islam. Therefore, idol seemed more appropriate as one that is worshipped and leads to *shirk*, both as a representation of god and an object of great love and admiration.
8. Claimed by Frances Pritchett to be an apocryphal verse inserted later, and not to be found in the original divans or poetry collections of Ghālib. Pritchett says: 'this verse is NOT by Ghālib. Even if you have heard it recited as such, even if in your heart you think it is, it's just not. Ghālib published his own divan four times, and we do know what he composed, and this verse is not his.' (http://www.columbia.edu/itc/mealac/pritchett/00ghalib/219/219_01.html?#apocryphal). Nonetheless, it is part of popular reception of the ghazal, and was sung by Jagjit Singh for Gulzar's eponymous TV series on Ghālib, and is retained here.

9   Written by Sahir at the conclusion of the Gandhi anniversary and the Ghalib centenary celebrations. Published in February 1970.
10 Note from the original: The reference is to 1969's terrible communal riots.
11 The poem was written when it was still illegal for women to drive in Saudi Arabia.
12 From the speech of Malala Yousafzai delivered at the UN youth assembly on 12 July 2013.
13 As recorded by Ramchandra Guha in *India After Gandhi*.
14 Edna St. Vincent Millay (1892–1950)—'What lips my lips have kissed, and where, and why, I have forgotten....'
15 Artemisia Gentileschi (1593–1656) was an Italian Baroque painter, one of the best in the generation after Caravaggio. She sought justice to no avail for her rape by the artist Agostino Tassi, but found artistic redemption in her paintings such as Judith slaying Holofernes where she is believed to have depicted the latter figure in Tassi's likeness.

FIRST PUBLICATION CREDITS

The Ghazal in Your Hands was first published in *Indian Literature*, 2017.

Ballimaran was first published in *Hastakshar*, 2009.

Restless—A Ghazal was first published in *Vayavya*, 2015.

This Night was first published in *40 Under 40*, 2016.

Scars or Gujarat and Kashmir was first published in *Muse India*, 2009.

View from Jama Masjid's Minar was first published in *Muse India*, 2009.

Feverish was first published in *The Ghazal Page*, 2016.

The L Word was first published in *The Four Quarters Magazine*, 2014.

Knowledge I was first published in *A Posy of Poesy*, 2009.

If I Could Write this in Fire was first published in *A Posy of Poesy*, 2009.

The Tall and Short of It was first published in *Postcolonial Text*, 2012.

Biryani in Belfast was first published in *Vayavya*, 2015.

Belfast/Béal Feirste was first published in *Postcolonial Text*, 2016.

On Those Nights was first published in *Writers Asylum*.

A Ghazal for Gaza was first published in *Economic & Political Weekly*, 2016.

Another Art was first published in *40 Under 40*, 2016.

Two Typos on Facebook was first published in *40 Under 40*, 2016.

The Summit of Cave Hill was first published in *Indian Literature*, 2017.

Merely a Heart—Trans. of a Ghazal by Ghalib was first published in *Muse India*, 2009.

Let's Live in that Place was first published in *Scroll.in*, 2016.

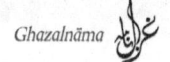
Ghazalnāma

Thousands of Desires Such was first published in *Scroll.in*, 2016.

Children's Play was first published in *Indiana Review*, 2017.

At Every Little Thing was first published in *Scroll.in*, 2016.

It Wasn't Our Destiny was first published in *Himal Southasian*, 2016.

Being was first published in *Scroll.in*, 2016.

Not a Wish Comes to Fruition was first published in *The Ghazal Page*, 2018.

To the Rival was first published in *Dhauli Review*.

Memory was first published in *Himal Southasian*, 2016.

Holi or The Lord's Holi was first published in *Scroll.in*, 2016.

Colour was first published in *Scroll.in*, 2016.

The Master of Royals was first published in *Scroll.in*, 2018.

The Heart is Asunder was first published in *Scroll.in*, 2018.

Somewhat was first published in *Scroll.in*, 2018.

Be it Gandhi, Be it Ghalib was first published in *Scroll.in*, 2016.

Air Black was first published in *Muse India*, 2017.

Muslimah was first published in *Muse India*, 2015.

In His Heart was first published in *Himal Southasian*, 2016.

Stardust was first published in *Scroll.in*, 2016.

A Shriek About Kashmir, July 2016 was first published in *Kashmir Lit*, 2016.

Let's War, Said He was first published in *City: A Journal of Literature & Ideas*. 2017.

The Frogs in Her Dreams was first published in *Indian Literature*, 2017.

Amaltas–Monsoon was first published in *Himal Southasian*, 2016.

Agra, 1948 was first published in *Economic & Political Weekly*, 2017.

Lessons in World Geography was first published in *Economic & Political Weekly*, 2017.

Caravans of Love was first published in *Indian Cultural Forum*, 2017.

Ghazal After Adrienne Rich was first published in *Indian Literature*, 2017.

ABOUT THE POET

Maaz Bin Bilal lived in Old Delhi for most of his life before leaving for a doctorate in literary studies at the Queen's University of Belfast. He now teaches at Jindal School of Liberal Arts and Humanities in Sonipat where he also lives when not back home in Delhi. Maaz also received the Charles Wallace India Trust Fellowship in Wales in 2018–19 for Writing and Translation. His translation from Urdu, *The Sixth River*, of Fikr Taunsvi's partition journal, is also out in 2019. *Ghazalnāma* is his first poetry collection.

www.ingramcontent.com/pod-product-compliance
Lightning Source LLC
LaVergne TN
LVHW030322070526
838199LV00069B/6533